MONOLOGUES: WOMEN

50 SPEECHES FROM THE CONTEMPORARY THEATRE

ROBERT EMERSON
JANE GRUMBACH
EDITORS

DRAMA BOOK PUBLISHERS
NEW YORK

First Edition

LIBRARY OF CONGRESS CATALOGING IN PUBLICATION DATA

Main entry under title:

Monologues—women.

1. Acting. 2. Monologues. I. Emerson, Robert. II. Grumbach, Jane.

PN2080.M56 808.82'45 76-1965

ISBN 0-910482-79-9

Manufactured in the United States of America

0 9 1 1 2 2 3 4 4 5 5 6 6 7 7 8 8 9 9 0 0

C O N T E N T S

ACKNOWLEDGMENTS

* * *

COMIC

BUTTERFLIES ARE FREE by Leonard Gershe

Jill -- 19 FEMALE — COMIC

A kooky girl tries to explain her philosophy of life.

I guess it was right after my marriage. I used to hang around Sunset Strip and smoke pot and say things like, "Down with the fuzz" and "Don't trust anyone over thirty." The whole bit. I just did it because everybody was doing it. Then I stopped because everybody was doing it. I felt I was losing my individuality -- whatever that is. The main thing, of course, was to protest against my mother, but it didn't work. I mean I walked in one day with my hair long and stringy, wearing far-out clothes and beads and sandals . . . she LOVED it! Next day, she had stringy hair and far-out clothes and beads and sandals. Well, I mean how can you protest against someone who's doing the same thing you are? Right? So, I went the other way and joined the Young Republicans for Ronald Reagan. Another mistake. There's no such thing as a young Republican.

SLOW DANCE ON THE KILLING GROUND by William Hanley

Rosie -- 19 FEMALE -- COMIC

Rosie, a plain-looking, unmarried girl with glasses, describes how she became pregnant.

If you knew me better, you'd see that this is exactly the kind of thing that's likely to happen to me. Getting knocked up, I mean. The point is it was my first time, I was a virgin before that. Wouldn't you know it, I'd get caught? Aside from everything else, I'm not lucky either. You see, if I was lucky, Harold and I could've succumbed to our silly little passion and that would've been that, the end of it. And New Rochelle, of all places. At least if it'd been in some nice apartment in the Village, say, with the sounds coming through the window of traffic and people, the breeze blowing the curtain over the bed, like in the movies. But, no. I lost my virginity in the attic of an old house in New Rochelle. Harold's grandmother's house. On a rainy day in spring on the floor of the attic in his grandmother's house, listening to the rain on the roof, breathing the dust of old things. . . . And what comes next but his grandmother who was supposed to be in the city for the day. But instead she's suddenly standing in the door to the attic, attracted there, no doubt, by the scuffling sounds of the imminent consummation. So she's standing there, screaming: (Rosie bangs on the table.) "Stop that! Stop that this instant!" Needless to say, it was out of the question. Stopping. At that particular moment. I mean, sex is like a flight over the sea, one reaches the point of no return. . . . I guess it sounds funny now, but, you know, at the time . . . it was pretty rotten. Sordid, I mean . . . it wasn't at all the way it's supposed to be. And Harold, of all people. A girl finds herself in this predicament, this condition, she'd at least like to be able to think of the cause of it as being some clever, handsome guy with charm and experience, just returned from spending a year in Rome, say, on a Guggenheim fellowship. But Harold, . . . Harold is six foot two, about a hundred and twenty five pounds, tops, an Economics major at CCNY . . . That's about the best I'll ever be able to do, I know it. (She smiles and snorts.) Ever since I found out I was pregnant I've been walking around with a face down to here and my mother kept saying, "What's the matter with you, anyway, I just don't know what's gotten into you lately." So, finally, I told her: a kid named Harold, as a matter of fact. . . . Oh, well, I just keep telling myself: "Remember Rosie, like in the song . . . Someday my prince will come . . . Snow White . . ."

BUS STOP by William Inge

Cherie -- 20 FEMALE -- COMIC

A singer tells how she was kidnapped by a cowboy.

Bo come in one night when I was singin' "That Old Black Magic." It's one a my best numbers. And he liked it so much, he jumped up on a chair and yelled like a Indian, and put his fingers in his mouth and whistled like a steam engine. Natur'ly, it made me feel good. Most a the customers at the Blue Dragon was too drunk to pay any attention to my songs. . . . I thought he was awful cute. . . . I'd never seen a cowboy before. Oh, I'd seen 'em in movies, a course, but never in the flesh . . . Anyway, he's so darn healthy lookin', I don't mind admittin', I was attracted, right from the start. But it was only what ya might call a sexual attraction. The very next mornin', he wakes up and hollers, "Yippee! We're gittin' married." I honestly thought he was crazy. But when I tried to reason with him, he wouldn't listen to a word. He stayed by my side all day long, like a shadow. At night, a course, he had to go back to the rodeo, but he was back to the Blue Dragon as soon as the rodeo was over, in time fer the midnight show. If any other fella claimed t'have a date with me, Bo'd beat him up. He kep tellin' me all week, he and Virge'd be by the night the rodeo ended, and they'd pick me up and we'd all start back to Montana t'gether. I knew that if I was around the Blue Dragon that night, that's what'd happen. So I decided to beat it. One a the other girls at the Blue Dragon lived on a farm 'cross the river in Kansas. She said I could stay with her. So I went to the Blue Dragon last night and just sang fer the first show. Then I told 'em I was quittin' . . . I'd been wantin' to find another job anyway . . . and I picked up my share of the kitty . . . but darn it, I had to go and tell 'em I was takin' the midnight bus. They had to go and tell Bo, a course, when he come in a li'l after eleven. He paid 'em five dollars to find out. So I went down to the bus station and hadn't even got my ticket, when here come Bo and Virge. He jest steps up to the ticket window and says, "Three tickets to Montana!" I din know what to say. Then he dragged me onto the bus and I been on it ever since. And somewhere deep down inside me, I gotta funny feelin' I'm gonna end up in Montana.

THE IMPORTANCE OF BEING EARNEST by Oscar Wilde

Gwendolen -- 20s FEMALE -- COMIC

Gwendolen does not react well when she discovers pretty, young Cecily is her fiance's ward.

(Raising her eyebrows.) Oh! It is strange he never mentioned to me that he had a ward. How secretive of him! He grows more interesting hourly. I am not sure, however, that the news inspires me with feelings of unmixed delight. I am very fond of you, Cecily; I have liked you ever since I met you. But I am bound to state that now that I know that you are Mr. Worthing's ward, I cannot help expressing a wish you were -- well, just a little older than you seem to be -- and not quite so very alluring in appearance. In fact, if I may speak candidly -- (Weighing her words.) Well, to speak with perfect candor, Cecily, I wish that you were fully forty-two, and more than usually plain for your age. Ernest has a strong upright nature. He is the very soul of truth and honor. Disloyalty would be as impossible to him as deception. But even men of the noblest possible moral character are extremely susceptible to the influence of the physical charms of others. Modern, no less than Ancient History, supplies us with many most painful examples of what I refer to. If it were not so, indeed, History would be quite unreadable.

THE PUBLIC EYE by Peter Shaffer

Belinda -- 22 FEMALE -- COMIC

Belinda tells her husband about her affair with the private eye he hired to follow her.

First let me tell you the oddest thing about this whole affair. I call it an affair because it is one. But do you know, for the whole three weeks since we first saw each other, we haven't exchanged a single word? When I say we meet every day, I don't mean we make a date. All I mean is that like Mary's little lamb, wherever I go he's sure to follow. He's a pure genius at following. You never see him till he decides to show himself. Then he just pops up -- click! Like that! -- in a coffee bar or a cinema, or out from behind a statue in the Park. Once I turned round and there he was in the Powder Room at Fortnum's. I suppose at the start I ought to have been scared, but I never was. Isn't that odd? All I knew was here was someone who approved of me. Who got pleasure out of just being in my company. Of course I realized he must be the loneliest man in town, but then in a way I was the loneliest girl, so it was sort of fitting. Who was I to complain if he got his kicks following me around?

After a bit -- and this is the really goofy thing -- I began to get mine by following *him*. The day came when he took over. I'd stopped outside a cinema where there was a horror film, and looked back as usual, just to make sure he'd seen me go in. And you know, he shook his head. He wasn't going to see that film. He was like you, you see: he didn't really like horror films. Mind you, he'd had a bit of a do with them: I'd made him sit through eleven that week. Instead he turned round, signed for me to follow and marched off to the next cinema. That was the first time I'd ever seen an Ingmar Bergman film. Charles, they're marvelous! This one had a poor old man driving all over Sweden in a motor car, looking for the turning he took wrong, years before. It's pathetic. It is really. At one point he saw himself in his own coffin! Anyway, as far as what you're thinking's concerned. After that the whole thing became marvellous. We never knew what each day would bring. Sometimes I would lead, sometimes he would. Last week I marched into the National Gallery and stopped in front of Bellini's Portrait of a Doge. He was terribly grateful: you know he'd obviously never seen it! He paid me back by leading me out to Syon House, which is hidden away behind all sorts of slummy things in Isleworth and has a huge hall of green marble, and twelve statues life-size in gold! I know everything about him now: what he likes doing, even the things he likes to eat -- and there are a great many of them. They're all sweet things -- he must be a Greek or something. Actually he looks a bit Greeky. And he knows everything about me. The other day we were in a shop and he laid out that -- (*She picks up the leather hat.*) for me to buy. And it's the only hat I don't look stupid in.

THE STAR-SPANGLED GIRL by Neil Simon

Sophie -- 23 (Southern) FEMALE -- COMIC

Sophie, new to New York, does not appreciate her neighbor's attentions.

Mr. Cornell, ah have tried to be neighborly, ah have tried to be friendly and ah have tried to be cordial . . . Ah don't know what it is that you're tryin' to be . . . That first night ah was appreciative that you carried mah trunk up the stairs . . . The fact that it slipped and fell five flights and smashed to pieces was not your fault . . . Ah didn't even mind that personal message you painted on the stairs. Ah thought it was crazy, but sorta sweet . . . However, things have now gone too far . . . Ah cannot accept gifts from a man ah hardly know . . . Especially canned goods . . . And ah read your little note. Ah can guess the gist of it even though I don't speak Italian. This has got to stop, Mr. Cornell . . . Ah can do very well without you leavin' little chocolate almond Hershey bars in mah mail box . . . They melted yesterday, and now ah got three gooey letters from home with nuts in 'em . . . And ah can do without you sneakin' into mah room after ah go to work and paintin' mah balcony without tellin' me about it. Ah stepped out there yesterday and mah slippers are still glued to the floor . . . And ah can do without you tying big bottles of Eau de Cologne to mah cat's tail. The poor thing kept swishin' it yesterday and nearly beat herself to death . . . And most of all, ah can certainly do without you watchin' me get on the bus every day through that high-powered telescope. You got me so nervous the other day ah got on the wrong bus. In short, Mr. Cornell, and I don't want to have to say this again, leave me ay-lone!

A THOUSAND CLOWNS by Herb Gardner

Sandra -- 25 FEMALE -- COMIC

A shy social worker decides to change the direction of her life by moving in with an eccentric client.

I didn't go to work this morning and I simply can't tell you how fantastic that makes me feel. I'm not going to do a lot of things any more. (Picks at the material of her blouse.) This blouse I'm wearing, my mother picked it out, everybody picks out things for me. She gets all her clothes directly from Louisa May Alcott. (Picks up stool, changes its position in the room.) Well, we've all seen the last of this blouse anyway. Do you realize that I feel more at home here after twenty-four hours than I do in my parents' house after twenty-five years? Of course, we'll have to do something about curtains -- and I hope you didn't mind about the screen around the bed; I just think it gives such a nice, separate, bedroomy effect to that part of the room -- Oh, there's so many wonderful tricks you can try with a one-room apartment, really, if you're willing to use your imagination -- I don't care if it sounds silly, Murray, but I was projecting a personality identification with the Statue of Liberty yesterday -- courageous and free and solid metal -- I was here with you last night and I don't give a damn who knows it or what anybody thinks, and that goes for Dr. Malko, Albert, my mother, Aunt Blanche -- Oh, I'm going to do so many things I've always wanted to.

LITTLE MURDERS by Jules Feiffer

Patsy -- 27 FEMALE -- COMIC

Just married, a girl has plans to change her husband.

Honey, I don't want to hurt you. I want to change you. I want to save you. I want to make you see that there is some value in life, that there is some beauty, some tenderness, some things worth reacting to. Some things worth feeling -- (Snaps fingers in front of his eyes.) Come back here! I swear, Alfred, nobody is going to kill you. But you've got to take some chances sometime! What do you want out of life? Just survival? It's not enough! It's not, not, not enough! I'm not going to have a surviving marriage, I'm going to have a flourishing marriage! I'm a woman! Or, by Jesus, it's about time I became one. I want a family! Oh, Christ, Alfred, this is my wedding day -- (Pause. Regains composure.) I want -- I want to be married to a big, strong, protective, vital, virile, self-assured man. Who I can protect and take care of. Alfred, honey, you're the first man I've ever gone to bed with where I didn't feel he was a lot more likely to get pregnant than I was. (Desperate.) You owe me something! I've invested everything I believe in you. You've got to let me mold you. Please let me mold you. (Regains control.) You've got me begging. You've got me whining, begging and crying. I've never behaved like this in my life. Will you look at this? (Holds out finger.) That's a tear. I never cried in my life. I never cried because I was too tough -- but I felt everything. Every slight, every pressure, every vague competition -- but I fought. And I won! There hasn't been a battle since I was five that I haven't won! And the people I fought were happy that I won! Happy! After a while. Alfred, do you have any idea how many people in this town worship me? Maybe that's the attraction -- you don't worship me. (Shakes head.) Maybe I'd lose all respect for you if you did all the things I want you to do. (Thinks on it.) Alfred, you've got to change! (Regains calm.) Listen. (Pause.) I'm not saying I'm better or stronger than you are. It's just that we -- you and I -- have different temperaments. (Explodes.) And my temperament is better and stronger than yours! (Frantic.) You're a wall! You don't fight! You hardly ever listen! Dear God, will somebody please explain to me why I think you're so beautiful.

FATHER'S DAY by Oliver Hailey

LOUISE -- 30s FEMALE -- COMIC

Married life was not a bowl of cherries for Tom and Louise.

Well, suppose I get it out in the open. Dear old Tom and I got a divorce because we didn't really care for one another. In the seven wonderful years we were married I struck him with brooms, mops, my electric curling iron -- assorted feminine apparatus. He swung at me with golf clubs, a baseball bat, a walking stick -- items of the male gender. I once tried to strangle him with my hair dryer cord. He tried it on me with his electric razor cord. When he was a little tight one night, I tried to force a swizzle stick down his throat. When he was sober enough, he tried that on me. I took that dangerous little plastic bag that comes from the dry cleaner's, tried my damnedest to hold it over his head. He then proceeded to have a suit cleaned -- not an original bone in his body -- and jumped me at the door one evening with his plastic bag. I tried to run him down with the car twice before he even figured out what I was doing. When he finally did figure it out, he tried to run me down with it. In short, it wasn't a good marriage. We got a divorce because we really didn't dig one another. And I hope to God I am typical -- and speak for most of the divorced people in this country -- when I say that is why we get divorced!

SCUBA DUBA by Bruce Jay Friedman

Jean -- early 30s FEMALE -- COMIC

Jean tries to explain to her white husband why she ran off with a black scuba diver.

Harold, will you just listen for a second? I'm not going to ask your full attention because I know I'm not entitled to that. Not in the short span of time that's been allotted to me on earth. But will you listen a little? I've been outside . . . All right, you know I've been outside, Harold. But what you don't know is that I looked around a little. And I saw what they're doing out there. They're not hollering out of windows, Harold. They're not taking their families three thousand miles to a beautiful new country with dozens of charming little villages to roam around in -- so they can stand around in bathrobes and shout things out of windows and never see those charming villages. Harold, let's face it. We both know there's only one charming thing in the world. You . . . in your bathrobe . . . shouting out of windows. That's the entire list. The charm line-up of our generation. . . . Let me tell you what happens to me when I'm outside, Harold. The strangest thing. You know how I trip a lot and bang my head on things and we both think it's cute although actually it's very serious and some of the injuries will probably turn malignant at a future date -- well, I don't trip over things out there. I didn't bang myself on the head once. There's nothing wrong with my eyes, Harold. I wish it were that. If it were an eye problem, believe me, I'd grab it. No, there's a reason that women out there don't bang into things and kill themselves. You see, they've had a breakthrough out there, Harold. They actually -- and you'd better sit down for this one -- they actually believe there's a difference between men and women. And here's the shocker of the year. You ready? They're doing something about it. They've come up with a separate way of treating women. They speak a little more gently to them. They actually say things to women. Romantic things. And it doesn't make them feel like Herbert Marshall either.

THE ICEMAN COMETH by Eugene O'Neill

Cora -- 30s FEMALE -- COMIC

A prostitute is not above supplementing her income by rolling drunks. Here she explains her method.

No, dis round's on me. I run into luck. Dat's why I dragged Chuck outa bed to celebrate. It was a sailor. I rolled him. (She giggles.) Listen, it was a scream. I've run into some nutty souses, but dis guy was de nuttiest. De booze dey dish out around de Brooklyn Navy Yard must be as turrible bugjuice as Harry's. My dogs was givin' out when I seen dis guy holdin' up a lamppost, so I hurried to get him before a cop did. I says, "Hello, Handsome, wanta have a good time?" Jees, he was paralyzed! One of dem polite jags. He tries to bow to me, imagine, and I had to prop him up or he'd fell on his nose. And what d'yuh tink he said? "Lady," he says, "can yuh kindly tell me de nearest way to de Museum of Natural History?" Can yuh imagine! At two a.m. As if I'd know where de dump was anyway. But I says, "Sure ting, Honey Boy, I'll be only too glad." So I steered him into a side street where it was dark and propped him against a wall and give him a frisk. (She giggles.) And what d'yuh tink he does? Jees, I ain't lyin', he begins to laugh, de big sap! He says, "Quit ticklin' me." While I was friskin' him for his roll! I near died! Den I toined him 'round and give him a push to start him. "Just keep goin'," I told him. "It's a big white building on your right. You can't miss it." He must be swimmin' in de North River yet! (With a business-like air.) I picked twelve bucks offa him. Come on, Rocky. Set 'em up.

LAST OF THE RED HOT LOVERS by Neil Simon

Jeanette -- 39 FEMALE -- COMIC

Jeanette's personal problems prevent her from committing adultery.

Do you know Charlotte Korman, big, red-headed, buxom woman, her husband is the Mercedes-Benz dealer in Wantagh? Mel doesn't like her. He doesn't want me to see her. He doesn't want her to be my friend, doesn't want her to come to our house; he can't stand Charlotte Korman. He's been having an affair with her for eight months! ~~I had to stop seeing her three times a week so he could see her four times a week. These are the times we live in, Barney~~. You know what my proof is? He told me. Two o'clock in the morning, he leans over, taps me on the shoulder and says, "I've had an affair with Charlotte Korman." Who asked him? When he tapped me on the shoulder in the middle of the night I thought he wanted me! ~~You know what it is to wake up from a sound sleep with no eyelashes and a dry mouth and hear that your husband is getting it from a woman you're not allowed to see for lunch?~~ And you know why he told me, Barney? He explained it to me. We're living in a new guiltless society. You can do anything you want as long as you're honest about it. Aren't we lucky to be living in such a civilized age? In the old days I would have gone to my grave ignorant of the wonderful and beautiful knowledge that my husband was spending his afternoons humping Charlotte Korman! . . . When he told me, I didn't say a word. I went down to the kitchen and made myself a cream cheese and jelly sandwich on date-nut bread. And that was the last time in eight months that I tasted food. . . . I estimate, going four times a week, I should be through with Doctor Margolies in another year. And then, when we both think I'm ready, I'm going to get in my car and drive off the Verrazano Bridge. In the meantime, I'm very depressed. Excuse me, Barney. Nothing personal, but I don't think we're going to have our affair.

THE KILLDEER by Jay Broad

Sparky -- early 40s FEMALE -- COMIC

Sparky describes the average day in the life of a housewife.

(Non-stop.) I got up, went to the bathroom, made breakfast, argued with you, threw my cup across the kitchen when you slammed the door as you went out, answered the telephone, Susan's car is broken, so I made the kiddie run, that's the third time this week, then I came back, washed the dishes, then Sparks and Mumsey called about coming to visit -- like you said they would -- then Frieda came over, we drank coffee, talked about her divorce, talked about her lawyer, talked about her alimony, then the bank called and I had to run down there to transfer out of our savings, that's wrong . . . to transfer what was left of our savings to cover your overdraft, then I came back and the phone rang again, it was Safeway telling me our grocery check had bounced, I told them to send it back through and the man said he would if I would bring him over two dollars to cover the redeposit cost, so I drove over to Safeway, I was very embarrassed but I did it anyway because I knew you wouldn't even if you said you would and I'd just have to answer the phone again tomorrow or start shopping somewhere else, then I heard screaming out on the street and I ran out, the Carlson's dog had been run over and nobody knew what to do, so I wrapped him in a towel and put him in the back of our car and drove over to the Vet's, he was dead when I got there and there was blood all over the back seat and there was nobody to help me get him out of the car except a smart little bastard who wanted to know why I brought a dead dog to the Vet's, then I came back here and cleaned the back seat, it's still wet, and the man came to give an estimate on the roof, it'll cost eight hundred and ninety dollars, not including any new spouts or gutters he may have to replace, I told him you'd call him tonight or tomorrow, and Georgia called, she was behind getting ready for the party and wanted to know if I'd do some shopping for her, I said OK, and back I went to Safeway, the groceries for Georgia came to fourteen something and all I had was ten, I asked if they'd take a check and we went through that whole thing again, but I promised and they did, and I took the groceries to Georgia, Susan was there and her car was still broken so I did the afternoon kiddie run for her, I came back here, Huck and Spike were home but Spike had gotten mad at Huck and locked him out, so Huck went over to Lynch's and got on the telephone and called Spike and told him he was a dirty fucker, so Spike came out and hit Huck in the nose, and by this time I was back but Spike had let the door close behind him and locked us all out and my keys were inside here on the counter so we had to break the lock on the garage window and Huck crawled in, and by that time I'd had my fill of one day on this green earth so I told them to make their own supper and I went over to have a drink with Georgia, but Marty was home and they were arguing over how many plates to put out for tonight's party, so I came back over here, closed the garage door, and sat in the car listening to the radio and drinking my martini . . . and it's the best twenty minutes I've had this year. Then I heard you come home, so I came in here and you were standing there shouting about the television . . . and you're lucky I didn't knock your teeth out . . .

SCENES FROM AMERICAN LIFE by A.R. Gurney, Jr.

Woman -- 40s FEMALE -- COMIC

A woman questions the feasibility of fencing in the neighborhood.

(Nervously.) Um. I want to make three quick points about this whole business of the fence. (Glances at first card.) Point one. Appearance. I don't like the looks of it. I know we've been having a lot of fires and robberies and terrorism, but I still don't like putting one of those ugly chain fences around the entire neighborhood. Even in the brochure, it looks terribly unattractive. That awful barbed wire. Those ghastly gates. I don't care how much planting or landscaping we do, we are still going to look like a concentration camp. And that's point one. (Next card.) Point two. Inconvenient. The whole thing is going to be terribly inconvenient. I hate the idea of having to get out of the car, to put my I.D. card into those gates just so they'll open and I can get home. And what about deliveries? How do the cleaners, and the milkman, and the eggman get in? The brochure simply doesn't say. (Next card.)

Point three, and then I'll sit down. What about dogs? This fence is electrified, remember. We can train our children to stay away from it, but what about dogs? Or do we have to tie them up? I refuse to do that, frankly. You know our Rosie, our old Lab. It would kill her to be tied up. I won't do it. And yet if Rosie should run up against this fence, she could be electrocuted. So what I suggest we do is, I suggest we call our friends in Shaker Heights, and Concord, and Palo Alto, and all the other places which have put in these fences, and we find out a few more details. I mean, I'm just not sure a fence is the best solution.

DOUBLE SOLITAIRE by Robert Anderson

Sylvia -- 40s FEMALE -- COMIC

Sylvia, a recent divorcee, explains her weekly schedule.

Mondays I see this movie bug. He has to sit near the screen, and his wife has to sit far back. For years they compromised and sat in the middle and spoiled it for both of them. Also, she is an easy weeper and cries at almost everything, which annoys him and makes him feel insensitive. And he laughs easily, which makes her feel she has no sense of humor . . . So . . . Tuesdays I see this man who loves games . . . particularly Scrabble. His wife thinks games are frivolous, and besides she can't spell . . . Wednesday is matinee day, and there's this sweet older man. He doesn't like to sit up late, so we have an early dinner after the matinee and I go home and get to bed early. A-lone. He's just had a heart attack, so that's why I'm free today . . . Thursdays I have lunch with this nice homosexual boy. That takes care of my mothering instincts . . . Thursday nights there's this man who likes to come and sit in my neat, pretty, attractive apartment . . . His sexual relations with his wife are marvelous, but she's a slob about her house. So he just comes and sits in my apartment and we talk. Each time he comes, he walks through my rooms and looks at them, shaking his head . . . Friday and Saturday nights are heavy date nights . . . Sundays I have The New York Times, and I do my other reading to keep up with the various interests of my dates . . . Scientific American . . . Art News . . . Cahiers du Cinema

. . . _Fortune_ . . . _Sports Illustrated_ . . .

THE GINGERBREAD LADY by Neil Simon

Evy -- 40s FEMALE -- COMIC

Evy tries to explain the hard facts of life to her daughter.

You're seventeen years old, it's time you judged me. I just don't want you to get the idea that a hundred and eighty-three pounds of pure alcohol is something called Happy Fat. . . . Many a night I would have thrown myself out that window if I could have squeezed through. . . . I'm not what you'd call an emotionally stable person. You know how many times I was _really_ in love since your father and I broke up? I met the only man who ever really meant anything to me about seven maybe eight times. Mr. Right I meet at least twice a week. . . . I sure know true love when I see it. It's wherever I happen to look. I want you to know everything, Polly, before you make up your mind. I lived here with that guitar player for eight of the happiest months of my life. Well, why not? He was handsome, funny, ten years younger than me, what more could a woman want? . . . He sat in that chair all day working and writing and I fed him and clothed him and loved him for eight incredible months. . . . And then that dirty bastard -- I'm sorry, I'm going to try not to do that anymore. No, the hell with it. That dirty bastard. He walked out on me in the middle of the night for an eighteen-year-old Indian hippie. "Princess-Screw-the-Other-Woman." . . . Wait'll she gets old and starts looking like the face on the nickel. And he doesn't have a penny, not a cent. Well, her moccasins'll wear out, we'll see how long that affair lasts. . . . But I sat at that window for six weeks waiting and hoping while I ran through two liquor stores in this neighborhood alone. . . . Finally Toby came in one day and found me face down in the bathtub. . . . I woke up in a sanitarium in Long Island, and the rest isn't very interesting unless you like stories about human torture. . . . But I went through it and I'm here. And I figure, pussycat, that I have only one more chance at this human being business . . . and if I blow it this time, they'll probably bury me in some distillery in Kentucky. . . . And if this is the kind of person you'd like to live with, God has cursed me with one of the all-time great schmucks for a daughter.

BYE BYE BIRDIE by Michael Stewart

Mother -- 50s FEMALE -- COMIC

A mother is very unhappy when her son plans to marry.

. . . So it's come at last! At last it's come! The day I knew would come at last has come at last! My sonnyboy doesn't need me anymore. Well, what are you waiting for? Get rid of me! (She indicates the garbage can.) Put me out with the garbage! Just throw me out with the used grapefruits and the empty cans from the Bumble-Bee salmon. Never mind putting a lid on. Leave it open so a hundred thousand pussycats can walk all over a Mother. And by the way, sweetheart darling, I got some good news for you. I got the report from the hospital. It's absolutely definite. I got a condition. Never mind what kind of condition, a condition. And the one thing doctors can't cure is a condition. I don't want you to worry though. Fancy funerals are for rich people. I don't want you to spend a cent. Just wait 'til Mother's Day, wrap me in a flag, and dump me in the river! (Then rising from garbage can.) Well. I feel better now. Everything is as it should be. A mother is lying on top of a Sanitation truck bound for the City Dump, and a son is running around in saloons with a Mexicali Rose who came over for the fruit picking season and stayed to ruin an American woman's life!

JEW! by Harvey Perr

Patti -- middle-aged FEMALE -- COMIC

While observing her daughter swim, Patti swills beer and complains about the neighbors.

Ard he, he comes storming out of his house with that old-bag wife of his -- I mean, did you ever see her legs? -- and he says -- and I must admit it was a graphic analogy -- that someone's got a hard on for his kids and he's gonna put a stop to it before there's an orgasm. (She addresses an unseen child.) Stop splashing, honey. Isn't it amazing how she takes to water, and only two years old. Throw a kiss to Aunt Hattie, Sugar. Kick your legs. Show Aunt Hattie how you swim. Isn't she too much? Look, look. At the other one. I guess you can tell she never learned manners of any sort, the way she stares and makes faces. Remember The Bad Seed? In spades! . . . Now you watch it in the deep end, you never can tell what maliciousness other children are capable of. Go on, kick your legs. Show 'em up. Ten years old and she acts younger than this sweet little two-year-old of ours. Drinks. Starts at ten ayem. That's ten in the morning. The both of them. And he has the nerve to call us alcoholics. A musician. He's a pothead, too. Why, his eyes like to pop sometimes, he's so stoned. Well no wonder his kids are, as you can see for yourself, so retarded morally . . . That's it. Keep splashing.

LOVERS AND OTHER STRANGERS by Renee Taylor & Joseph Bologna

Bea -- middle-aged FEMALE -- COMIC

A woman and her daughter-in-law are looking at the wedding album.

And Joan, of all the pictures in your wedding album, my favorite is this one. The whole family together. Everyone happy and smiling. You and Richie, me and Frank, your mother and father, and Richie's cousins -- Freddie and Rita, cheek to cheek; David and Loretta, kissing; Carmel and Vinnie, hugging -- Freddie and Rita, cheek to cheek. Did you know that Freddie has not said one word to Rita for two years? . . . But they're still together. David and Loretta, kissing -- Well you know what people in the family say about David, that he's a little funny? You know what I mean? Peculiar. I don't think he really is. It's just his way to lock himself in his room all day Sunday and play with his cars. Look, it takes all kinds to make a world. Who's to say the man is a degenerate, or worse? But they're still together! Carmel and Vinnie, hugging . . . When Carmel and Vinnie first got married, they lived with Vinnie's parents because he was out of work a lot and Vinnie's mother was always picking on Carmel. She kept blaming Carmel for Vinnie's laziness. Well, one night Carmel told Vinnie if his mother made one more remark to her, she was going to smack her in the face and Vinnie started yelling, "Don't you dare lay a hand on my mother!" and Carmel said, "Oh, go to hell, the both of you!" and she stomped out of the house and Vinnie chased her down the block and dragged her back by the hair and Carmel spit right in his face and he started choking her by the throat over the open window and the super had to come and pull Vinnie off Carmel . . . and they're still together. (BEA sits back obviously pleased with herself.)

SERIOUS

A WOMAN OF NO IMPORTANCE by Oscar Wilde

Hester -- 20s FEMALE -- SERIOUS

Hester is disgusted by the double-standard practiced by society.

Lord Henry Watson! I remember him, Lady Hunstanton. A man with a hideous smile and a hideous past. He is asked everywhere. No dinner-party is complete without him. What of those whose ruin is due to him? They are outcasts. They are nameless. If you meet them in the street you would turn your head away. I don't complain of their punishment. Let all women who have sinned be punished. It is right that they should be punished, but don't let them be the only ones to suffer. If a man and woman have sinned, let them both go forth into the desert to love or loathe each other there. Let them both be branded. Set a mark, if you wish, on each, but don't punish the one and let the other go free. Don't have one law for men and another for women. You are unjust to women in England. And till you count what is a shame in a woman to be an infamy in a man, you will always be unjust, and Right, that pillar of fire, and Wrong, that pillar of cloud, will be made dim to your eyes, or be not seen at all, or if seen, not regarded.

FLINT by David Mercer

Dixie -- 20s FEMALE -- SERIOUS

Cradling her baby, Dixie tries to explain to the police her relationship to a recently killed Anglican minister.

No, sir. I have no means of support. (Pause.) The father? (Pause.) No father. (Pause.) I had a friend who -- (Pause.) He was killed in an accident. Drove his motorbike into an army truck full of something explosive. (Pause.) Somewhere abroad, you know. (Pause.) He couldn't see properly. It was the sun. (Pause.) In his eyes. (Pause.) And he was old. An old man. (Pause.) No, sir, he was not the father. (Pause.) Edna Mary Cecilia O'Keefe. (Pause.) It was a terrible explosion. Nothing left of my man. My friend, I mean. In the fire. (Pause.) What a fire! They couldn't get near. (Pause.) The child's name is Prometheus, sir. That was my friend's idea. No, I've never heard anything like it myself, either. (Pause.) But we agreed on it before he was born. (Pause.) I agreed with my friend on all matters of importance, though you could not say he was an easy man to understand. And is now, I should think, frying in a greater fire than that so tragically laid on by the army. Whoever's army it was. (Pause.) He will be amazed to find himself in hell. Though he had a wicked sense of humour, and I fancy will hold his own in his own quaint way. With the Devil. (Pause.) In my ninth month he would lay his hand on my belly and sing. This little song. (Pause.) He nicknamed Prometheus here, Prom. (Pause.) Prom is quite nice, isn't it? (Pause.) I would lie in my nightshift in those hotels in those foreign places. And my friend would sing with his hand on my bulge. In his quavering voice. A poor singer, for a man of the church. But that would be his vocal cords I think. Do the vocal cords go quicker than other parts of the anatomy? Well he would quietly sing, sir. And he brought me a fine, wholesome peace. (She sings.)

Pom tiddley om pom -- Prom Prom;
Prom tiddley om pom -- Pom Pom --
etc.

INHERIT THE WIND by Jerome Lawrence & Robert E. Lee

Rachel -- 20s FEMALE -- SERIOUS

After years of being dominated by her preacher father, Rachel finally decides to leave him and lead her own life. (The book she refers to is "The Origin of Species" by Darwin.)

I'm going away. I'm leaving my father. Bert, it's my fault the jury found you guilty. Partly my fault. I helped. This is your book, Bert. I've read it. All the way through. I don't understand it. What I do understand, I don't like. I don't want to think that men come from apes and monkeys. But I think that's beside the point. Mr. Drummond, I hope I haven't said anything to offend you. You see, I haven't really thought very much. I was always afraid of what I might think -- so it seemed safer not to think at all. But now I know. A thought is like a child inside our body. It has to be born. If it dies inside you, part of you dies, too! (Pointing to the book.) Maybe what Mr. Darwin wrote is bad. I don't know. Bad or good, it doesn't make any difference. The ideas have to come out -- like children. Some of 'em healthy as a bean plant, some sickly. I think the sickly ideas die mostly, don't you, Bert?

THE WATERING PLACE by Lyle Kessler

Janet -- 20s FEMALE -- SERIOUS

Janet explains why she stays continuously pregnant.

Everyone was eating . . . drinking . . . talking. I stood up. I felt ill. I tried to go upstairs. It was impossible. The staircase was jammed. There was no room to move . . . no air to breathe. Someone cried out! I thought I heard a cry. It came from outside. Someone was crying outside. I pushed my way to the door. The cry was louder now. It was a scream. I looked out. It was dark. I could see nothing. I turned around and ran in. I rushed back into the room. The sound was unbearable. It was closer now, louder, it was in the room. No one moved. They were silent. They were watching me. All of their eyes were on me. What's the matter with you? Don't you hear it? I yelled. Don't you hear that scream? I cupped my hands over my ears to drown out the awful sound of it . . . and then for the first time I understood why no one else but I heard it. The scream was not coming from without but from within, from within me, from deep within my flesh. It was my child who was screaming, my infant who was suffocating. The sound I heard was the terrible agony of its death. I fainted. When I woke up I was in the hospital. The baby was dead. He was born dead. Mother went to pieces. She could accept Ronald's death, but not this, not the two deaths one after the other. It was Father's idea . . . the pillow. When Mother saw me pregnant again she calmed down. Father said it would only be for a day or two . . . until she regained her strength, until she was strong enough to accept the truth. If I listened to him I would be here forever. I would remain nine months pregnant the rest of my life.

MIDDLE OF THE NIGHT by Paddy Chayefsky

The Girl -- 24 FEMALE -- SERIOUS

The Girl explains her marital problems to her boss.

You know what my husband would do if he came in like you just did and found me breaking down like I just did, do you know what he'd do? He'd turn on the television set, do you know what I mean, Mr. Kingsley? Or else he'd invite the neighbors in. Anything except sit down with me and talk things out. Oh, I'm not being fair to him. He tried, he really tried, but I tried too. I tried everything. You just can't imagine how naive I was about marriage, Mr. Kingsley. I really thought you lived happily ever after. Look, Mr. Kingsley, if I sound like I'm blaming my husband, I don't want to sound that way. This is me. I wanted poor George to make up for everything I never had in my life. I wanted him to be my father and my mother -- my father ran away when I was six years old. Oh, Mr. Kingsley, here I go again. You'd better get out of here because I've been building up all day like a volcano. Did you ever go downtown in the afternoon by the Paramount Theater? Did you ever see those fourteen, fifteen-year-old kids hanging around, cutting school. They're the loneliest looking kids in the world. Well, that's just what I was like when I was a kid. I used to go to the Paramount three or four times a week. I didn't cut school though. I was always very good in school. Can I get you something to eat or drink, Mr. Kingsley? I don't know what we have in the house. I haven't eaten all day, but do you know what I mean by lonely kids, Mr. Kingsley? (Begins to cry again.) I'm sorry, Mr. Kingsley, but just seeing you sitting there, listening to me -- Boy, you came here just to pick up a couple of sales slips. Oh, Mr. Kingsley, I'm so glad you came -- My husband, George, the last couple of months we've hardly talked to each other. He comes home and I ask him what happened during the day. He always says, "Nothing." We never eat home anymore. We go to a restaurant and we just sit there, eating. He doesn't know what to do with me, do you know what I mean? I'm his wife, so he comes home for dinner. But it's nothing, do you know what I mean? There's no love or anything. Well, I can't stand that. I want him to love me. I want him to be pleased to see me. I want him to come home and tell me all that's happened to him and how he feels about things. And I want to tell him how I feel. I -- I want something. I mean, is this what marriage is? Is this what life is? Boy, life isn't much if that's what it is.

BIRDBATH by Leonard Melfi

Velma -- 26 FEMALE -- SERIOUS

Velma confesses that she murdered her mother.

NOOOOOOO! (She pulls a small kitchen knife out of her pocketbook. It is partly caked with dry blood.) YOU STAY AWAY FROM ME! I DON'T WANT YOU TO TOUCH ME! We're not even married yet . . . You leave me alone, Frankie . . . or I'll kill you! When . . . we got up this morning, my mother and me, we had coffeecake and caviar for breakfast. It was a big surprise. My mother said that we were havin' the treat even if payday was three days away yet. She said it was sort of a special celebration. My mother said that she was leaving for the mountains this afternoon. She was going to a resort to meet a man. Harriet, my mother's friend who lives in the next apartment, she told my mother that there were a whole lot of available men at this certain resort up in the mountains, the Catskills, I think, and my mother said she was goin' no matter what, and that I must send her money every weekend until she has some luck. She said that I couldn't go because I would scare the men away, that I would ruin her chances, and that I was really such an ugly girl, and that I looked like the mother and she looked like the daughter . . . and then she said that was why we're havin' the treat early: to celebrate! The coffeecake and caviar . . . and then she asked me to cut her a big piece of the coffeecake and to cover it with a whole lot of caviar . . . and so I started to cut the coffeecake with this here knife, but . . . It's my mother's blood! I didn't know what to do. I don't . . . know why I did it! I don't even really remember that much, Frankie. When I got in the subway to come to work afterwards it was jist like nuthin' happened, nuthin' at all! But do you know? I thought, I thought when my mother asked me to cover her piece of coffeecake with a whole lot of caviar, I thought . . . my mother . . . she thinks that my head is a hammer! That's what she thinks! AND IT ISN'T! IT ISN'T! Tell me, Frankie, please tell me that my head is not a hammer!

THE SIGN IN SIDNEY BRUSTEIN'S WINDOW by Lorraine Hansberry

Iris -- 29 FEMALE -- SERIOUS

An actress tells of the horror of auditioning.

You don't know what it's like though -- God, to walk through those agency doors. . . . There's always some gal sitting on the other side, at a desk, you know, with a stack of pictures practically up to the ceiling in front of her. And they're always sort of bored, you know. Even the polite ones, the nice ones, I mean, they've seen five million and two like you and by the time you come through that door they are bored. And when you get past them, into the waiting room, there they are -- the five million and two sitting there, waiting, and they look scared and mean and as competitive as you do. And so you all sit there, and you don't know anything: how you look, how you feel, anything. And least of all do you know how they want you to read. And when you get inside, you know less. There are just those faces. Christ, you almost wish that someone would make a pass or something; you could deal with that, you know -- that's from life. But that almost never happens, at least not to me. All I ever see are those blank director-producer-writer faces just staring, waiting for you to show them something that will excite them. . . . And you just stand there knowing that you can't, no matter what, do it the way you did it at home in front of the mirror, the brilliant imaginative way you did it the night before. And all you can think is: What the hell am I doing standing here in front of these strangers, reading these silly words and jumping around for that fairy like some kind of nut . . . ? Sidney, I wish I had it in me to -- be tougher. Like -- like Gloria, I guess.

CAT ON A HOT TIN ROOF by Tennessee Williams

Margaret -- 30 FEMALE -- SERIOUS

Maggie tries to convince her husband that his best friend (now dead) was a homosexual.

I know, believe me, I know that it was only Skipper that harbored even any unconscious desire for anything not perfectly pure between you two! You married me early that summer we graduated out of Ole Miss, and we were happy, weren't we, we were blissful, yes, hit heaven together ev'ry time that we loved! But that Fall you an' Skipper turned down wonderful offers of jobs in order to keep on bein' football heroes -- pro-football heroes. You organized the Dixie Stars that Fall so you could keep on bein' team-mates forever! But somethin' was not right with it! -- Me included! -- between you. Skipper began hittin' the bottle . . . you got a spinal injury -- couldn't play the Thanksgivin' game in Chicago, watched it on TV from a traction bed in Toledo. I joined Skipper. The Dixie Stars lost because poor Skipper was drunk. We drank together that night all night in the bar of the Blackstone and when cold day was comin' up over the Lake an' we were comin' out drunk to take a dizzy look at it, I said, "SKIPPER! STOP LOVIN' MY HUSBAND OR TELL HIM HE'S GOT TO LET YOU ADMIT IT TO HIM!" -- one way or another! He slapped me hard in the mouth! -- then turned and ran without stoppin' once, all the way back to his room at the Blackstone. That night, when I came to his room that night, with a little scratch, like a shy little mouse at the door, he made that pitiful, ineffectual little attempt to prove that what I had said wasn't true. In this way, I destroyed him, by telling him truth that his world which he was born and raised in, had taught him couldn't be told! From then on Skipper was nothin' at all but a receptacle for liquor an' drugs. Who shot Cock Robin? I -- with my merciful arrow! Brick, Brick, I'm not tryin' to whitewash my behavior, Christ, no! Brick, I'm not good. I don't know why people have to pretend to be good, nobody's good. The rich or the well-to-do can afford to respect moral patterns, conventional moral patterns, but I never could afford to, yeah, but I'm honest! Give me credit for just that, will you, please? Born poor, raised poor, expect to die poor unless I can manage to get us something out of what Big Daddy leaves when he dies of cancer! But, Brick! Skipper is dead! I'm alive! Maggie the Cat is alive! I'm alive, alive!

FATHER'S DAY by Oliver Hailey

Estelle -- 30s FEMALE -- SERIOUS

Estelle is having a hard time adjusting to her divorce.

I admire Marian very much. At the orphanage, the biggest battle they had with us was self-pity. They were always having people come and talk to us about it. I usually didn't listen. I'd put my fingers in my ears. Who needed it -- right? I only remember one old guy -- I think he was a Lutheran or something -- but I remember him because he didn't try to kid us. Everybody else was always telling us it didn't matter whether we had a mother or a father -- it wasn't that important. He said hell yes it mattered. Face it, we'd gotten a lousy break -- but that was the way it was. A husband, a wife, a set of kids -- life doesn't always work out that neatly. Sometimes all you get is an aunt in Dubuque who might come and get you next year. Bits and pieces. So what you have to do is take those bits and pieces and -- only then I put my fingers in my ears again. Because I knew what I was going to do. I was going to get out of that place and get married and raise a family and no bits and pieces life for me. Only this evening I lost my husband -- really lost him -- and the twins are going to love her -- and love meeting all the DuPonts -- who wouldn't? -- and so I'm back to bits and pieces again. Only Marian's shown me what you do with them. You take them and you put them together as best you can. Of course there'll always be people to tell you you can't. You can't make a life that way. Lives aren't made that way. Well, you're wrong, Louise. Lives are made every way. The thing to do is to keep them going. And not to hate. Marian doesn't hate. I'm not going to, either. I wish you wouldn't.

A LOSS OF ROSES by William Inge

Lila -- 30s FEMALE -- SERIOUS

A small-time actress remembers a moment from her childhood.

I remember my first day of school. Mother took me by the hand and I carried a bouquet of roses, too. Mama had let me pick the loveliest roses I could find in the garden, and the teacher thanked me for them. Then Mama left me and I felt kinda scared, 'cause I'd never been any place before without her; but she told me Teacher would be Mama to me at school, and would treat me just as nice as she did. So I took my seat with all the other kids, their faces so strange and new to me. And I started talking with a little boy across the aisle. I din know it was against the rules. But Teacher came back and slapped me, so hard that I cried, and I ran to the door 'cause I wanted to run home to Mama quick as I could. But Teacher grabbed me by the hand and pulled me back to my seat. She said I was too big a girl to be running home to Mama and I had to learn to take my punishment when I broke the rules. But I still cried. I told Teacher I wanted back my roses. But she wouldn't give them to me. She shook her finger and said, when I gave away lovely presents, I couldn't expect to get them back . . . I guess I never learned that lesson very well. There's so many things I still want back.

RASHOMON by Fay & Michael Kanin

Wife -- 30s FEMALE -- SERIOUS

Raped by a bandit, a wife must now defend herself against her husband's hatred.

He's gone -- He's gone -- and we're still alive! (Suddenly, she is overcome by hysterical sobs and laughter, and it is with difficulty that she collects herself.) Forgive me -- it's only because I'm so grateful -- I watched your hands cutting against the rope till the blood came. How horrible it must have been for you, my husband. But I want you to know -- he couldn't hurt me -- all his coarseness, all his brutality -- because I thought only of our life together. He couldn't touch that. I'll forget it, my love. I promise you. And we'll go on as we -- Your eyes -- What is that I see in them? (Shaking her head in growing horror.) No -- you can't mean it! (Covering her face with her hands.) I won't look! I won't! (She starts to cry. Suddenly she rises, picks up his sword and holds the handle out to him.) Here -- take it and kill me! If that's how you feel, kill me! (Anguished.) Kill me! But don't look at me with such -- contempt -- Not even that. You are cruel. I never knew any man but you -- I never wanted one. I didn't ask for this to happen to me -- What do you want me to do? Go away and never see you again? Where would I go? What would I do -- without you? (Suddenly her pride rebels.) Answer me. Am I so low that you can't throw me a word -- like a bone to your dog? Answer me! I am no longer the daughter of a maidservant in your house. I am your wife! I've shared your table and your bed! Answer me! Answer me! (Hysterically.) Answer me! Answer me -- !

SNOWANGEL by Lewis John Carlino

Connie -- 30s FEMALE -- SERIOUS

A prostitute remembers her one true love.

(She staggers through a few dance steps and sings to the tune of "Frankie and Johnny.") Connie and Johnny were lovers. Lordy how they could love. Swore to be true to each other. To be . . . true . . . (Her expression clouds. She seems to drift.) He came to me while I was workin' in a house in Stockton. His name was Paco. He'd come up from the mountains in the south of Mexico ta dig potatoes. I turned a coupla tricks with him. Short times. He was always so quiet . . . and . . . I don't know, kinda gentle. Then he came in one day and paid for the price of a day's work. He took me out into the country. We sat down on a hillside, in the sunshine. He had a bottle of dago red. He started ta talk ta me. It was all fast and crazy at first. Then I understood. It was about his home. There were lakes where men fished with nets in the shape of great, huge butterflies. There were old temples and big snakes and everybody played the guitar and sang and had a helluva good time. And he laughed when he tole me. And the sun hit his teeth. He had a smile that made ya feel like butter. Damn, he had a smile! We drank the wine and he went on about the fruits and the colors of things and how great it was ta live with animals, and about all the beautiful churches with gold and silver crosses and saints that came from Spain in the olden days. And the mountains are so high, the snow never melts. Then he said, "Connie, I take you to my home. Caramba, when they see you they will fall down dead. Beautiful. They have never seen such beautiful. Caramba, mi vida, you will be the sun and the music and the fire of my house. You will be my blanket. Then you will do this work no more. And we will forget. Ay, Caramba, Connie, we will forget." An' he'd laugh. Damn, he had a smile. We lay in the sun all day. An' you know what? He kissed me gently . . . so gently. An' he touched my hair. "Caramba, Connie, how we will forget." He dug his nails inta dirt for a whole week ta buy that day. I waited, but he never came back. Immigration got him. He'd snuck in. They sent him back. I didn't even know his last name. I never saw him again. Little Paco. Paco the Mex. I never loved anybody again. I got busted after that and went to Frisco. And then, after that . . . that was all. That's what I remember, mister. That's what I imagine.

A CLEARING IN THE WOODS by Arthur Laurents

Virginia -- 30s FEMALE -- SERIOUS

Tormented by the past, Virginia comes home to try to piece her life together.

Eight days ago, I went to my office, to the same door that I have been opening for over three years -- The door was not locked, Barney. But I could not open it. I could not make my hand touch the knob! I pretended to be searching my purse as one of the secretaries opened the door for me. The next evening, I couldn't open the door to my apartment. I pretended to the superintendent that I had forgotten my key. Then I couldn't open the closets and I told my maid to leave them open, I wanted everything aired. I started to go to a doctor but I was ashamed; I knew there was nothing physically wrong. Then, in my office, I could not even open the drawers in my desk. I sat, day after day, staring at the sign with my name on it telling me who I was. When someone came in, I picked up the telephone and recited jargon. When alone, I began staring at the open window . . . I dropped a piece of paper out, then a cup, then an ashtray. My office is on the sixteenth floor now. Yesterday I took off my shoes and crouched on the window sill. How long? (Shakes her head.) Sense of time and place have gone. Then one of the phones rang like an air raid alarm -- and I ran. To my apartment? Yes, because I had wedged a piece of cardboard in the door so it would stay open -- and there was a breeze from the river. The bathroom curtains were moving and I was standing in the ugly light of the medicine chest. The bottle of sleeping pills was on the sink and I opened it with my teeth. Then -- then I was running: down halls and stairs. Then riding, no, driving down a houseless road that stopped at a footpath through the trees. The path, I knew; the path brought me here: home. Why isn't it pretty here? (Smiles.) Probably because that absurd feeling has followed me. That something terrible is going to happen to me.

THE DAYS BETWEEN by Robert Anderson

Barbara -- 30s FEMALE -- SERIOUS

A wife fights against her husband's desire to leave her and his job.

(Suddenly flaring.) All right, go! Go ahead! You're gone. Go to your God damned freedom. But I won't come to see if you've killed yourself . . . because I'll know . . . without coming, I'll know that you have killed yourself. Because you will . . . when you have nothing but time and freedom and nobody to blame . . . What are you going to write about? What? . . . Tell me. You don't know anything about life. You hate life . . . this life, this ugly but only life. . . . And you cannot write from hate, only from love, and you . . . you are incapable of love or loving. You can only hate and rape! . . . Yes, it has been rape, but I wanted to be warm and open and ready. . . . Do you know, do you have the faintest idea what it does to a woman not to want her husband? . . . But you have crucified us all on this dream of yours! (She becomes almost hysterical.) You're sick . . . and I'm sorry as hell for you . . . but I hate you and I won't take the blame any more . . . and I don't give a good God damn what happens to you. I killed a child for you. Yes . . . I killed a child for you. . . . For your dream. . . . A child in my body . . . I did. . . . For you. . . . Yes, for you. You killed the child. Your hatred. Your dream. For you. I loved you . . . I loved you . . . and it was for you, so that you could be free! (She is hysterical now.) Well, you're free now. Go ahead! Go to Nancy! Go to your glorious freedom -- I don't give a damn!

A MOON FOR THE MISBEGOTTEN by Eugene O'Neill

Josie -- 30s FEMALE -- SERIOUS

Josie, an over-sized farm girl, cradles a drunken James Tyrone to her breast.

That's right. Do what you came for, my darling. It isn't drunken laughter in a speakeasy you want to hear at all, but the sound of yourself crying your heart's repentance against her breast. She hears. I feel her in the moonlight, her soul wrapped in it like a silver mantle, and I know she understands and forgives me, too, and her blessing lies on me. There. There, now. You're a fine one, wanting to leave me when the night I promised I'd give you has just begun, our night that'll be different from all the others, with a dawn that won't creep over dirty windowpanes but will wake in the sky like a promise of God's peace in the soul's dark sadness. (She smiles a little amused smile.) Will you listen to me, Jim! I must be a poet. Who would have guessed it? Sure, love is a wonderful mad inspiration! Asleep. (In a tender crooning tone like a lullaby.) That's right. Sleep in peace, my darling. (Then with sudden anguished longing.) Oh, Jim, Jim, maybe my love could still save you, if you could want it enough! (She shakes her head.) No. That can never be. God forgive me, it's a fine end to all my scheming, to sit here with the dead hugged to my breast, and the silly mug of the moon grinning down, enjoying the joke!

JOE EGG by Peter Nichols

Sheila -- 35 FEMALE -- SERIOUS

Sheila, the mother of a spastic child, has trouble with her

husband too.

One of these days I'll hit him. Honestly. (Brushes hair, looks at audience.) He thinks because he throws a tantrum I'm going to stay home comforting him and miss the rehearsal and let them all down. He thinks he's only got to cry to get what he wants. I blame his mother. She gave him the kind of suffocating love that makes him think the world revolves around him but because he's too intelligent to believe it really, he gets into these paddies and depressions. And when he's in one of those, he'll do anything to draw attention to himself. That beetle on his face -- you saw that. And all this stuff about Freddie. And yet it was Brian made me join these amateurs in the first place, he said I needed to get out more, have a rest from Joe. But she's no trouble. It's Brian. I don't know which is the greatest baby. Watching somebody as limited as Joe over ten years, I've begun to feel she's only one kind of cripple. Everybody's damaged in some way. There's a limit to what we can do. Brian, for instance, he goes so far -- and hits the ceiling. Just can't fly any higher. Then he drops to the floor and we get self-pity again . . . despair. I'm sure, though, if he could go farther -- he could be a marvellous painter. That's another reason I said I'd join the amateurs: the thought that he'd be forced to go upstairs several nights a week and actually put paint on canvas. And even if he isn't any good, he seems to need some work he can be proud of. Something to take his mind off his jealousy of anyone or anything I take to . . . relatives, friends, pets . . . even pot-plants. I'm sure it's because they take up time he thinks I could be devoting to him. And Joe, most of all, poor love . . . (She puts brush on table or chair. A thought brings her back.) Look, you mustn't assume I feel like this in the ordinary way. And even when I am a bit down, I shouldn't normally talk about it to a lot of complete strangers. But all this childish temper over Freddie -- this showing-off -- it's more than I can stand, it makes me boil, honestly! Wouldn't you feel the same? (Checks her appearance in imaginary full-length glass.) That's why I'm telling you all this. A lot of total strangers. But wouldn't it make you boil? Honestly! A grown man jealous of poor Joe --

ORPHEUS DESCENDING by Tennessee Williams

Lady -- 35-45 FEMALE -- SERIOUS

Lady tells her lover that she is pregnant.

You gotta go now -- it's dangerous for you to stay here. . . . Take your pay out of the cash-box, you can go. Take the keys to my car, cross the river into some other county. You've done what you came here to do. . . . I have life in my body, this dead tree, my body, has burst in flower! You've given me life, you can go! When a woman's been childless as long as I've been childless, it's hard to believe that you're still able to bear! -- We used to have a little fig tree between the house and the orchard. It never bore any fruit, they said it was barren. Time went by it, spring after useless spring, and it almost started to -- die. . . . Then one day I discovered a small green fig on the tree they said wouldn't bear! I ran through the orchard. I ran through the wine-garden shouting, "Oh, Father, it's going to bear, the fig tree is going to bear!" -- It seemed such a wonderful thing, after those ten barren springs, for the little fig tree to bear, it called for a celebration -- I ran to a closet, I opened a box that we kept Christmas ornaments in! -- I took them out, glass bells, glass birds, tinsel, icicles, stars. . . . And I hung the little tree with them, I decorated the fig tree with glass bells and glass birds, and silver icicles and stars, because it won the battle and it would bear! (Rises, ecstatic.) Unpack the box! Unpack the box with the Christmas ornaments in it, put them on me, glass bells and glass birds and stars and tinsel and snow! Because I've won, I've won, Mr. Death, I'm going to bear!

SWEET BIRD OF YOUTH by Tennessee Williams

Princess -- middle-aged FEMALE -- SERIOUS

Her young lover has called Princess's old friend, Sally Powers, to further his career, but Princess has different ideas.

-- Why did I give him the number? Well, why not, after all, I'd have to know sooner or later, so why not now, after all . . . I started to several times, picked the phone up, put it down. Well, let him do it for me. Something's happened. I'm breathing freely and deeply as if the panic was over. Maybe it's over. He's doing the dreadful thing for me, asking the answer for me. He doesn't exist for me now except as somebody making this awful call for me, asking the answer for me. The light's on me. He's almost invisible now. What does that mean? Does it mean that I still wasn't ready to be washed out like an algebra problem, unfinished, is washed off a blackboard by a wet sponge when the -- closing -- bell rings? He said a whore. He means I made a whore of him. That doesn't exist for me now, nothing exists for me, now, but the call he's making for his own crazy purpose. Poor boy! I pity him: do I? -- Maybe . . . But one thing's sure. It's only the call I care for. I seem to be standing in light with everything else dimmed out. He's in the dimmed out background as if he'd never left the obscurity he was born in. I've taken the light again as a crown on my head to which I am suited by something in the cells of my blood and my body from the time of my birth. It's mine, I was born to own it, as he was born to make this phone-call for me, to Sally Powers, dear Sally Powers, dear faithful custodian of my -- out-lived legend. The legend that I've out-lived. . . . Monsters don't die early: they hang on long. Awfully long. Their vanity's infinite: almost as infinite as their disgust with themselves . . .

CAMINO REAL by Tennessee Williams

Marguerite -- 40s FEMALE -- SERIOUS

Caught in the shadowy existence of Camino Real, Marguerite remembers the past.

Oh, Jacques, we're used to each other, we're a pair of captive hawks caught in the same cage, and so we've grown used to each other. That's what passes for love at this dim, shadowy end of the Camino Real. . . . What are we sure of? Not even of our existence, dear comforting friend! And whom can we ask the questions that torment us? "What is this place?" "Where are we?" -- a fat old man who gives sly hints that only bewilder us more, a fake of a Gypsy squinting at cards and tea-leaves. What else are we offered? The never-broken procession of little events that assure us that we and strangers about us are still going on! Where? Why? and the perch that we hold is unstable! We're threatened with eviction, for this is a port of entry and departure, there are no permanent guests! And where else have we to go when we leave here? Bide-a-While? "Ritz Men Only"? Or under that ominous arch into Terra Incognita? We're lonely. We're frightened. We hear the Streetcleaners' piping not far away. So now and then, although we've wounded each other time and again -- we stretch out hands to each other in the dark that we can't escape from -- we huddle together for some dim-communal comfort -- and that's what passes for love on this terminal stretch of the road that used to be royal. What is it, this feeling between us? When you feel my exhausted weight against your shoulder -- when I clasp your anxious old hawk's head to my breast, what is it we feel in whatever is left of our hearts? Something, yes, something -- delicate, unreal, bloodless! The sort of violets that could grow on the moon, or in the crevices of those far away mountains, fertilized by the droppings of carrion birds. Those birds are familiar to us. Their shadows inhabit the plaza. I've heard them flapping their wings like old charwomen beating worn-out carpets with gray brooms. . . . But tenderness, the violets in the mountains -- can't break the rocks!

MOURNING BECOMES ELECTRA by Eugene O'Neill

Christine -- 40s FEMALE -- SERIOUS

Christine fears that her daughter and son may have discovered she killed their father.

Vinnie, I -- I must speak with you a moment -- now Orin is here. I appreciate your grief has made you -- not quite normal -- and I make allowances. But I cannot understand your attitude toward me. Why do you keep following me everywhere -- and stare at me like that? I had been a good wife to him for twenty-three years -- until I met Adam. I was guilty then, I admit. But I repented and put him out of my life. I would have been a good wife again as long as your father had lived. After all, Vinnie, I am your mother. I brought you into the world. You ought to have some feeling for me. (She pauses.) Don't stare like that! What are you thinking? Surely you can't still have that insane suspicion -- that I -- (Then guiltily.) What did you do that night after I fainted? I -- I've missed something -- some medicine I take to put me to sleep -- Oh, you did -- you found -- and I suppose you connect that -- but don't you see how insane -- to suspect -- when Doctor Blake knows he died of -- ! (Then angrily.) I know what you've been waiting for -- to tell Orin your lies and get him to go to the police! You don't dare do that on your own responsibility -- but if you can make Orin -- Isn't that it? Isn't that what you've been planning the last two days? Tell me! Answer me when I speak to you! What are you plotting? What are you going to do? Tell me!

SUMMERTREE by Ron Cowen

Mother -- 40s FEMALE -- SERIOUS

A mother tries to describe the pain of losing a son to war.

You know, when it comes, you think it's going to be a terrible surprise, that you'll tear it up or wad it into a little ball, that you'll scream or go insane. Or at least cry. But you don't. You know it's happened before the telegram arrives. Something in your mind heard the clicks of the teletype machine addressing you as "Dear Mr. and Mrs. so-and-so," and adding its deepfelt regrets, before you even see the paper. I went out in the back yard and sat down in the grass under the tree. It's been years since I've sat in the grass. So I sat there and I thought back to when we had this Irish Setter . . . her name was Ginger. Her full name was Gingerella of Brianwood -- the only royalty I've ever met. It was funny to be thinking about an old dog at a time like that, but that's what I was thinking. I remembered how I used to pretend I was crying because it would upset her. She'd run over and jump on me -- and she was a very big dog -- and she'd whine and lick my face. She really thought I was crying. Then I would burst out laughing and push her away. One day she got sick and I had to take her to the vet. He said she would have to stay there, and to take her upstairs where he had a room full of cages where he kept the dogs. Ginger was so sick she could hardly get up the stairs. I tried to help her, but all my pushing and pulling probably hurt her more. When we got into the room, all the dogs started barking and jumping around. It scared Ginger and she tried to run away. But she could hardly move. So she just cried. I led her into her cage and then I ran down those stairs, so glad to be away from there. I never saw Ginger again. She died, and I guess they tossed her into the incinerator somewhere. I never cried until that day in the back yard. (Pause.) And I don't even know if I was crying for Ginger . . . or my Son.

LONG DAY'S JOURNEY INTO NIGHT by Eugene O'Neill

Mary -- 54 FEMALE -- SERIOUS

Mary, now completely under the influence of drugs, reminisces about her youth.

(Staring dreamily before her. Her face looks extraordinarily youthful and innocent. The shyly eager, trusting smile is on her lips as she talks aloud to herself.) I had a talk with Mother Elizabeth. She is so sweet and good. A saint on earth. I love her dearly. It may be sinful of me but I love her better than my own mother. Because she always understands, even before you say a word. Her kind blue eyes look right into your heart. You can't keep any secrets from her. You couldn't deceive her, even if you were mean enough to want to. (She gives a little rebellious toss of her head -- with girlish pique.) All the same, I don't think she was so understanding this time. I told her I wanted to be a nun. I explained how sure I was of my vocation, that I had prayed to the Blessed Virgin to make me sure, and to find me worthy. I told Mother I had had a true vision when I was praying in the shrine of Our Lady of Lourdes, on the little island in the lake. I said I knew, as surely as I knew I was kneeling there, that the Blessed Virgin had smiled and blessed me with her consent. But Mother Elizabeth told me I must be more sure than that, even, that I must prove it wasn't simply my imagination. She said, if I was so sure, then I wouldn't mind putting myself to a test by going home after I graduated, and living as other girls lived, going out to parties and dances and enjoying myself; and then if after a year or two I still felt sure, I could come back to see her and we would talk it over again. (_She tosses her head -- indignantly_.) I never dreamed Holy Mother would give me such advice! I was really shocked. I said, of course, I would do anything she suggested, but I knew it was simply a waste of time. After I left her, I felt all mixed up, so I went to the shrine and prayed to the Blessed Virgin and found peace again because I knew she heard my prayer and would always love me and see no harm ever came to me so long as I never lost my faith in her. (_She pauses and a look of growing uneasiness comes over her face. She passes a hand over her forehead as if brushing cobwebs from her brain -- vaguely_.) That was in the winter of senior year. Then in the spring something happened to me. Yes, I remember. I fell in love with James Tyrone and was so happy for a time. (_She stares before her in a sad dream_.)

A FAR COUNTRY by Henry Denker

Amalie -- old FEMALE -- SERIOUS

Freud's mother fears her son will end up a failure as her husband did.

Listen to me! I'll tell you things that can happen to a human being. Yes! The night we had to abandon our home in Freiburg. I was a wife. And a mother, with Sigmund by the hand, you here. (_Touches her stomach_.) And yet not more than a child myself. (_Gets handkerchief out of muff_.) We stood on the railroad platform late at night. Misty, cold. Papa carrying two small valises, everything we owned in the world. And he kept staring down the track, searching for the train. But only to avoid facing me. Because his little weaving mill failed we had to give up our home. Had to go to a strange and hostile city. I couldn't help being terrified. Even the poverty I knew in Freiburg seemed better than the uncertainty of Vienna. But I told myself, you must not cry. He feels badly enough. Then the sound of the train whistle cut through the night and I -- when I heard the whistle -- saw the light of the train -- felt its grinding roar rushing at me I wanted to hurl myself under it! I will save them from the fear and the disappointments! I tightened my hold on Sigmund so he could not get away from me. And I moved forward till I felt his little hand suddenly grow ice cold in mine -- as though he sensed -- and then I -- I couldn't do it -- couldn't. But for that, you might have died before you were even born. I don't want you to live through anything like that.

SUNRISE AT CAMPOBELLO by Dore Schary

Sara -- old FEMALE -- SERIOUS

Sara cautions her crippled son, Franklin Delano Roosevelt, against trying for the Presidency.

I wonder if you truly know what is good for you. You come by your Dutch stubbornness by birth. And some of that Dutch stubbornness is mine, from long association. Franklin, many years ago, when I was a little girl, I sailed to China with my father on Clipper ships. On one of those trips, many years ago, as we rounded Cape Horn we headed into a fearful storm. My father, eager and headstrong, urged the Captain to head into the sea, to fight through the storm. But fortunately the Captain of the ship was a better sailor than my father. He wanted to save his ship. He gave orders to trim sails and heave to! We rode out the storm safely, and when the heavy weather was gone, we were able to sail ahead and nothing was lost, nothing. Be wise, Franklin. Ride out the storm. Son, what do you believe I want for you? Obscurity, invalidism? Do you believe that this is my ambition for you? Having been a mother for over forty years, do you think this is what I want? Any dream you ever had or could have, I have. All pain you have felt I have felt. I don't want to see you hurt.

ANASTASIA by Marcelle Maurette, adapted by Guy Bolton

EMPRESS -- old FEMALE -- SERIOUS

The former Empress of Russia believes she has found her long lost granddaughter.

Malenkaia! Malenkaia! Malenkaia! I couldn't believe it at first. You've come from so far away and I waited and waited and waited. Don't cry -- don't say anything -- you are warm, you are alive -- that is enough. I can stand no more for now. Can't you hear how that weary old heart of mine is beating? I must go -- but don't be afraid -- I shall come back -- I need you. Let go of my dress. That is what you used to do as a child. Be sensible, Malenkaia. I'll go as I used to -- speaking to you as I left the side of your little bed. We will go, tomorrow if you like, to my old palace in Finland. It is still there and still mine. There is a very old man there -- our lamplighter. Each evening he goes from one room to another lighting the empty lamps -- until for him the great dark rooms are ablaze with light. The other servants take no notice -- they realize that he is childish. And perhaps that is true of us all -- and we are lighting dead lamps to illumine a life that is gone. Goodnight, Anastasia -- and please -- if it should not be you -- don't ever tell me --

SERIO-COMIC

ORPHEUS DESCENDING by Tennessee Williams

Carol -- 30s FEMALE -- SERIO-COMIC

Carol explains her new philosophy of life.

I used to be what they call a Christ-bitten reformer. You know what that is? -- A kind of benign exhibitionist. . . . I delivered stump speeches, wrote letters of protest, about the gradual massacre of the colored majority in the county. I thought it was wrong for pellagra and slow starvation to cut them down when the cotton crop failed from army worm or boll weevil or too much rain in summer. I wanted to, tried to, put up free clinics, I squandered the money my mother left me on it. And when that Willie McGee thing came along -- he was sent to the chair for having improper relations with a white whore -- I made a fuss about it. I put on a potato sack and set out for the capitol on foot. This was in winter. I walked barefoot in this burlap sack to deliver a personal protest to the Governor of the State. Oh, I suppose it was partly exhibitionism on my part, but it wasn't completely exhibitionism, there was something else in it, too. You know how far I got? Six miles out of town -- hooted, jeered at, even spit on! -- every step of the way -- and then arrested! Guess what for? Lewd vagrancy! Uh-huh, that was the charge, "lewd vagrancy," because they said that potato sack I had on was not a respectable garment. . . . Well, all that was a pretty long time ago, and now I'm not a reformer any more. I'm just a "lewd vagrant." And I'm showing the "S.O.B.'S" how lewd a "lewd vagrant" can be if she puts her whole heart in it like I do mine! All right. I've told you my story, the story of an exhibitionist. Now I want you to do something for me. Take me out to Cypress Hill in my car. And we'll hear the dead people talk. They do talk there. They chatter together like birds on Cypress Hill, but all they say is one word and that one word is "live," they say "Live, live, live, live, live!" It's all they've learned, it's the only advice they can give. -- Just live. . . . Simple! -- a very simple instruction.

AND MISS REARDON DRINKS A LITTLE by Paul Zindel

Anna -- 30s FEMALE -- SERIO-COMIC

Anna tells her neighbor why she has given up religion.

I was teaching at Jefferson which was in the other direction from where Catherine was, so I had to depend upon this teacher Faith Farber, a crippled teacher whose father is a Christian Scientist which is the reason Faith Farber is a cripple -- well, Faith Farber was driving me to school which used to drive me crazy watching her twisted leg search for the gas pedal. I had to watch the road closely because her reflexes are so bad sometimes she used to put on the windshield wipers instead of the brakes . . . And we were driving by Mr. Fisher's Mobil gas station when this little puppy comes running right out in front of the car, but we stopped in time. And there's this cute little puppy looking at me sitting in Faith Farber's suicide seat, and he's wagging his tail a mile a minute and looking so grateful . . . then, the puppy decides to go back the way he came, which is right in front of me in the death seat, when this big trailer truck comes zipping along right there, right out my window, and I yelled out: NO, PUPPY! NO, PUPPY! And the truck driver sees what's going on and he jams on his brakes but the front wheels come to a stop right on the back half of this little puppy, squirting his guts across the road. I let out a scream, and the little puppy is still alive, his legs rammed out toward me, his eyes looking right at me -- and he's saying: EHHHHHHHH! EHHHHHHH! And then the truck moves ahead and the back wheels go right over the puppy's head and paws and the rest of it, and there's only this little wet spot on the road. And Mr. Fisher, old, poor Mr. Fisher, whose wife had died the year before -- old Mr. Fisher comes running out of his Mobil service station and he took one look and passed out banging his head on the concrete. That was the last day I wore crosses.

FATHER'S DAY by Oliver Hailey

Marian -- 30s FEMALE -- SERIO-COMIC

Marian explains why she prefers being divorced.

That's wonderful, Estelle. Because I must tell you, unlike marriage, divorce just gets better and better and better. I just can't imagine a . . . better existence. You see, when we were married, I was forever wondering, is Richard sleeping with someone else too? I suppose I knew he was. He always did, he always will. Anyway, I'd keep wondering what are the others like? Are they blonde? Are they a little dumpy? And then one evening I came in unexpectedly. I'd gone to Boston with my father -- he was scheduled to give a lecture there -- but a bunch of fascists protested and his talk was cancelled all of a sudden. So we came back the same night. And when I entered the bedroom and flipped on the light, there they were. Only Richard flipped the light off again so quickly I didn't get a good look at her. So we were divorced and I still didn't know what they looked like. And then one night a few months later Richard called and took me to dinner. And afterwards he took me to bed. And suddenly in the middle of it, I knew what they looked like -- all those women he was taking to bed. They had long, lovely legs. (She runs a hand across her own long, lovely legs.) Long, lovely hair. (Another hand flicks across her long, lovely hair.) And faces of almost patrician beauty. (She holds her head high and proudly.) They looked like me -- of course. And at that moment I had my first orgasm.

LAST OF THE RED HOT LOVERS by Neil Simon

Elaine -- late 30s FEMALE -- SERIO-COMIC

Accused of taking their proposed, but not yet consumated, extra-marital affair too lightly, Elaine flys into a rage.

You hypocrite! You soul-searching, finger-smelling, hypocritical son of a bitch! Who are you to tell anybody how to go through life? What would you have done if I came in here all fluttery and blushing and "Ooh, Mr. Cashman, don't put your hand there, I'm a married woman"? Were you going to tell me how much you respect me, admire me and, at the moment of truth, even love me? You know damn well tomorrow you'd be back behind that counter opening clams and praying to Christ I'd never come back in your restaurant. And you know something? That's the way it should be. Forgive me for the terrible, sinful thing I'm about to say but I happen to like the pure physical act of making love. It warms me, it stimulates me and it makes me feel like a woman -- but that's another ugly story. That's what I came up here for and that's what you were expecting. But don't give me, "When I was nine years old my mother ran off with the butcher and I've been looking for someone to love me ever since." I don't know your problems and I don't care. Keep your savory swordfish succotash stories to yourself. No one really cares about anything or anyone in this world except himself, and there's only one way to get through with your sanity. If you can't taste it, touch it or smell it, forget it! If you want a copy of that speech, send fifty cents and self-addressed envelope --

THE SUBJECT WAS ROSES by Frank D. Gilroy

Nettie -- 45 FEMALE -- SERIO-COMIC

Nettie tells her son why she married his father.

I think it was his energy . . . a certain wildness. He was not like my father at all . . . I was attracted . . . and I was afraid. I've always been a little afraid of him. . . . And then he was clearly a young man who was going places. Twenty-four when I met him and making well over a hundred a week. Great money in those days and his prospects were unlimited. . . . Money was never plentiful in our house. We weren't poor like his people, you understand. Never without rent, or food, or tickets to the opera, or nice clothes. But still we weren't well to do. . . . My father brought home stories from the hotel about the various bigwigs who came in and what they wore and how they talked and acted. And we went to the opera. And we had friends who were cultured. Musical Sunday afternoons. Those were papa's happiest moments. . . . Yes, I liked good things. Things that the baker from Paterson and the others could never give me. . . . But your father surely would. The way he was going he would be a millionaire. . . . That was his dream, you know -- to be a millionaire by the time he was forty. . . . Nineteen twenty-nine took care of that. He was never quite the same afterwards. . . . But when I met him he was cock of the walk. Good looking, witty young Irishman. Everyone liked him, and those who didn't at least feared him because he was a fierce fellow. Everyone wanted to go into business with him. Everyone wanted to be social with him. . . . He was immediately at home on a ship, a train . . . in any bar. Strangers thought he was magnificent. And he was . . . as long as the situation was impersonal. . . . At his best in an impersonal situation. . . . But that doesn't include the home, the family. . . . The baker from Paterson was all tongue-tied outside, but in the home he would have been beautiful. . . . Go to bed now.

SALVATION ARMY by Robert Patrick

Reba -- 50s or 60s FEMALE -- SERIO-COMIC

A mother tells her son about her childhood in rural Texas.

Well, to start with, everybody worked -- grown-ups and children, everyone -- and I guess we weren't children, ever, the way you were. We pulled weeds and swept floors and I did dishes and Becky tended the vegetable garden and helped with the baby, and your Uncle Harry, from the time he was small, was handy with a hammer and saw, and Saturday, well, Saturday was the one day we were ever, ever, let feel like a child. I remember even thinking that, when we were dressed up, "Now I look like a little girl from the magazine pictures, yes." And we'd get in the wagon -- oh, once the baby peed on Becky and she couldn't get out of the wagon to go to the picture show -- she just had to sit there in the wagon -- and she cried that whole Saturday -- even when Harold and I brought her her ice-cream cone. The ice-cream, oh, yes, that was the big thing. That was the crowning moment of the week. We each got a dime -- whenever times were good -- and one nickel of it was for the picture show (They were very short then and didn't have much of a story) -- and that was very exciting -- but the ice-cream cone -- that was what the other nickel was for -- the ice-cream cone -- and I remember one Saturday -- I saw a lady eating a dish of ice cream when I went in to get my cone -- and on top of it was a bright red maraschino cherry -- and I was just -- oh! I had to have that! -- so I hopped up on a stool -- it was so high -- stools aren't that high anymore -- because ladies' dresses were so long -- and I said: "I'll have a dith of ithe cream pleathe, mithter," and he laughed and they all made me say it again -- and finally he gave me the saucer of ice cream, no more than you'd get in a cone, but with that cherry -- and I gave him my dime and picked up my spoon -- and he put my dime in the old beautiful black cash-register covered with gold scrolling and he rang it up -- and I held out my little hand for my nickel change -- and he just walked past me down to the other end of the counter -- and I looked up and the little tab in the cash-register window said "10 cents!" And I hadn't known that ice cream in a dish at the counter cost a whole dime -- and that meant I wouldn't get to see the picture show -- and I didn't even get to have a cone -- they were wonderful in those days, they were covered with scrolling as elaborate as the cash register -- and so I picked up the spoon -- and I was crying, the front of my little dress was wet, tears were running out of my eyes -- and I started to eat that one dip of ice cream -- and I savored every drop -- and I took so long it was all melted before long -- and I scooped it out of every corner of that saucer, and I licked both sides of the silver spoon -- and the sun was slanting in the window, and in came my Daddy and Becky and Harold and the baby looking for me, and I knew they were going to tease me for crying and because I needed help to get down off the stool, and because I hadn't come to the picture show -- but first they had to watch me, with my tiny little silver spoon, eat that big, bright, red maraschino cherry -- and -- do you know? -- I stole the spoon.